TELLING THE OLD, OLD STORY

TELLING THE OLD, OLD STORY

In a Postmodern World

STEPHEN BURNHOPE

Foreword by Andy Kind

TELLING THE OLD, OLD STORY
In a Postmodern World

Inquiries to the author may be addressed to steveburnhope@gmail.com.

 A catalogue record for this book is available from the National Library of Australia

Publisher
Adiaphora Publications
91A High Street
Great Missenden
HP16 0AL
United Kingdom

PAPERBACK ISBN: 978-1-3999-2132-9
EBOOK ISBN: 978-1-7397095-0-1

Print and Distribution: Ingram & Lightning Source (UK/ US/ EUR/ AUS)

TABLE OF CONTENTS

FOREWORD

Gaudete, gaudete
Christus est natus
Ex Maria virgine, gaudete
Tempus ad est gratiae hoc quod optabamus
Carmina laetitiae devote redamus

THIS SIXTEENTH-CENTURY CHRISTMAS CAROL, made famous and eerie by folk leviathans Steeleye Span, contains some of the most truthful and beautifully communicated words ever written about Jesus Christ, don't you agree? Oh, you don't speak Latin and therefore the words are meaningless. Well please don't blame me for your inadequate schooling ...

I'm one of those people who believes that Christianity is true; that it's the best story out there, the most faithful rendition of whatever symphony the universe is playing. No human mind can fully grasp objective reality, but knowing ultimate truth is a different matter: when ultimate truth turns out to be a person, it becomes a case of who you know, not what you know.

However, truth still needs to be communicated in meaningful terms. It simply isn't enough to throw biblical catchphrases at people in the hope of convicting them. 'The wages of sin is death,' reads a billboard on the side of a desolate articulated truck parked in a field, overlooking the M56 motorway. I agree with that statement, but it's meaningless if the person hearing or reading those words doesn't know what sin means or doesn't have a basic grasp of payroll systems.

It is possible to communicate the right words in the wrong way with the right intention. When I was in High School, I played Hamlet in a school production. I learned the words by rote and belted out 'To be or not to be' in my most forceful oratory. I had no idea what the speech was about—none at all. It wasn't until I saw the actor Andrew Scott playing the same role a few years later that I realized it's a speech contemplating suicide. Same speech, different meaning. Acting is not simply presenting—it's incarnating.

Words *do* have meaning. But the meanings of words change over time. Truth may always be fixed, rooted somewhere below the surface soil and gritty sediment of interpretation and caricature, but digging down to get at that truth isn't easy without someone or something to help you dig. This book, then, is a massive spade. It removes boulders of dogma, slices through the stolid clay of cliché and, ultimately, exhumes from the ground something that many evangelical Christians have lost or never really had in the first place: a proper understanding of what we talk about when we talk about the Gospel.

Atonement, salvation, sin, covenant—all words that modern Christians can lob around with reckless abandon, when perhaps they should be handled with care. Until we learn how to translate them into our cultural context, the truth of these words will remain buried and become increasingly fossilized, because people don't know what they mean.

Filtering the Gospel into our cultural context isn't the same as diluting it. You can throw a whole melon into a hippo's mouth with no problem; if you want humans to enjoy it, though, you need to break it down into chunks and bring out the Parma ham.

Appropriately, it is with forensic care and surgical calmness that Steve Burnhope (Dr Burnhope to his friends—just 'Professor,' to me) unpicks all these terms without unravelling people's confidence in the Gospel. Indeed, what remains when the whole is stitched back together is a tapestry that is both logically consistent and aesthetically pleasing—and I don't know many theologians who can do that.

You will find in this book the same pastoral gentleness, the same unpatronizing patronage, that I have found from knowing the real man over the past decade or so. Steve is fond of picture language, so let me use the analogy of Gandalf leading the brave yet terrified hobbits through the dark, murky subterranean chambers of Moria—a vast labyrinthine network of tunnels and mines under the Misty Mountains in Middle-earth. That captures fairly accurately the impact he has had on my theology and Christian journey, and how you may well feel reading this book. Steve's stance as a writer is the same as his approach to ministry: to lead without dragging, to persuade without manipulating.

I am confident that you will find this book short and to the point, helpful, and illuminating. Will you enjoy it? Well, as Steve himself might say, it all depends on what we mean by 'enjoy.' But yes, you will enjoy it.

It's a rare book where nothing is lost in translation.

Rejoice, rejoice!
Christ is born of Mary,
Rejoice!
The time of grace
that we have waited for is here.
Let's sing for joy!

ANDY KIND
Comedian, preacher, and author
Head of Evangelism, Youth for Christ, UK
April 2022

INTRODUCTION

I love to tell the story
'Twill be my theme in glory
To tell the old, old story
of Jesus and His love.[1]

—— ARABELLA KATHERINE HANKEY, 1866

THE 'OLD, OLD STORY' of the Gospel is central to Christian faith and especially so within evangelicalism. Not all readers may be familiar with that word, but it's a broad-brush term for a loosely-connected worldwide movement of Protestant churches that identify themselves as centered on the Gospel—the Greek word for which is *euangelion*.

What exactly it means to be an evangelical is often debated, not least in the light of more than three-quarters of voters who self-identified as (white) evangelicals voting for Trump in the 2016 and 2020 US Presidential elections.[2] But setting that to one side, those debating its definition and boundaries have often settled for a version of the so-called 'Bebbington Quadrilateral'—British historian David Bebbington's proposal that historic evangelicalism has had four special hallmarks as its irreducible common features: Biblicism, Crucicentrism, Conversionism and Activism.[3]

What that means in ordinary language is that (1) evangelicals honor the Bible which contains the Gospel story as a divinely-inspired text, uniquely authoritative for life and faith; (2) the cross of Christ is the central and crucial event in the story (the word 'crucial' deriving from 'the cross'); (3) there is a need for individuals to experience personal 'conversion' in response to the story; and (4) evangelicals must be active in proclaiming the story and seeking responses.

Given that need for a personal response, evangelicalism (at its most successful) is conscious that its Gospel message must relate well to a specific cultural context. In other words, it must be presented sufficiently thoughtfully to 'make sense' to its hearers in a particular location, historical period, and cultural setting, since however much 'truth' a message may contain, that is of little use if the people to whom it's addressed can't grasp it.

And yet, there is a self-evident tension between communicating the message in language and ideas with which people in a culture can identify and capitulating to that culture by changing the message to make it more amenable. As Bebbington explains, this tension is nothing new:

> The deepest divisions in the evangelical world generally arose from the impact of the cultural waves. Deep-seated theological debates ... were usually about whether truth was being compromised by the intellectual trends of the times. The assimilation of new ideas was naturally unsettling.[4]

The challenge has been exacerbated in the past half century by Western society becoming ever-more Postmodern in its worldview. Evangelicalism began in the Protestant Reformation, coterminous with Modernity. Its ways of thinking (its 'obviouses' about life, faith, and the Bible) have been shaped and formed within that worldview. In the present day, however, it now has to contend with overlapping worldviews, as the Modernity that reigned supreme (until the 1950s) has been increasingly giving way to Postmodernity. It is easy to see how evangelical concerns as to how to engage with the culture but also stand against the culture can lead to diametrically different responses to such a change—which in turn impact on how we think about communicating the Gospel.

The not-uncommon belief that Postmodernity 'threatens' Christianity often leads to a perception that evangelicals need to mount a defense based on the way in which the Gospel has been understood and presented in Modernity. Typically, this means referring back to the language and ideas of the Protestant Reformers, often becoming intertwined with references to 'tradition,' 'traditional beliefs,' and 'traditional values.' The concerns are understandable, but it's all too easy to confuse an unchanged Gospel with an unchanging set of phrases, cultural assumptions, and images to convey that Gospel (especially when we're talking about a set that's of relatively recent vintage in the history of Christianity). If we are to communicate with and within a culture, we need to speak the language of that culture. This is far more than just changing our vocabulary—though that will be needed as well—and it's certainly not just trying to look and sound 'cool.' It's centered on culturally situated, culturally aware ways of thinking. We will not win people to the Gospel if what we say 'does not compute' for them—if they 'don't get it'—truth or no truth.

So, cultural contexts change; but bottom line, the question is to what extent do we, today, have a mandate to change how we present and explain the Gospel in response to the cultural environment in which we find ourselves? What constitutes 'change'? What is timeless in the way the 'Old, Old Story' has been told, and what was time-bound in the past? What does the word 'biblical' mean in this context?

The answers to these questions must start by bringing into conversation what we see in the Bible with what has happened in Christian history.

Surprising though it might seem, the ways in which the Gospel has been conveyed over the past two millennia have evolved quite considerably, reflecting that identified need for it to have 'made sense' to its hearers in different locations, historical periods, and cultural settings. An awareness of how and why that evolution came about will provide the basis for us, today, to continue in that same tradition, for the same reasons.

The historical perspective is, therefore, where we will start the journey.

1

THE OLD, OLD STORY IN HISTORICAL PERSPECTIVE

DEFINING OUR TERMS

THE WORD GOSPEL COMES from an Old English word, *godspel*, which is a combination of two separate words: *god*, meaning 'good,' and *spel*, meaning 'news' or 'story.' So, before the Old, Old Story is anything else, it starts with being good news: the Gospel is a 'good news story.' This helps explain why we call the first four books in the New Testament the Gospels. They're different perspectives, from different angles—Matthew's take, Mark's take, Luke's take and John's take—on why and how Jesus of Nazareth is good news.

This, then, is our first 'takeaway.' If the way in which we're explaining the Old, Old Story to people isn't sounding like good news, it may be time to rethink how we're telling it. No-one will be persuaded by a Gospel that sounds like bad news, or no news, or irrelevant news. Since we know that Jesus is good news—and the original story was good news—the problem can lie only in its transmission. Something must have happened to the story in the journey from 'then' to 'now.'

The question of, how, exactly, Jesus is good news, is answered theologically by reference to another word—'atonement.' The doctrine of atonement is answering the 'How?' question of salvation. In other words, we believe that Jesus saved us ... but how, exactly? We believe he saved us through the cross ... but how, exactly? Every time we ask and answer 'How?' questions of salvation, we're talking about the atonement. The word itself comes from Middle English, and it means to be made 'at one' with someone: brought into a state of 'at—one—ment.' Atonement is about a restored relationship: reconciliation between people and God. It's relational, not 'transactional.'

> Therefore, if anyone is in Christ, the new creation has come: the old has gone, the new is here! All this is from God, who reconciled us to himself through Christ and gave us the ministry of reconciliation: that God was reconciling the world to himself in Christ, not counting people's sins against them. And he has committed to us the message of reconciliation. 2 Corinthians 5.17-19

That 'message of reconciliation' is the Gospel. Atonement is explaining how that reconciliation, that restored relationship, has been brought about. The 'ministry of reconciliation' that Paul references here is everyone's calling to participate in, as evangelical Christians. It's not about 'getting' saved, or 'getting' salvation— nor even, 'getting to heaven.' We will say more about that word atonement a bit later, but in the first instance it's being brought into a reconciled relationship with God through Jesus, from which everything else then flows.

THE OLD, OLD STORY IN THE CREEDS

Given the obvious importance of the atonement, it's really quite surprising that the classic Creeds of the early church which define orthodox Christianity—in other words, what we need to believe, to be 'proper' Christians—make no mention of it. They talk about forgiveness of sins, but they're silent on how that comes about. They talk about the incarnation (God becoming man), and Jesus' suffering, and his death and resurrection, but they're silent on what role each of those played. The early Church Fathers speak about all sorts of benefits imparted by Jesus, but nowhere do they coordinate their main ideas or attempt to sketch a rationale of salvation.[5]

Why might that have been? We don't know. One reason might be that they all thought it was so 'obvious' at the time that no-one needed to memorialize it in a Creed; which is a great shame, from our perspective, 2,000 years later. A more likely reason might be because there was never any controversy about it. Much of the material in the Creeds came about because of various heresies that were going around, to formally clarify what Christians ought to believe. So far as we know, there was nothing about atonement they felt the need to pronounce on, in the way they did in relation to, say, the divinity and humanity of Jesus in the Chalcedonian Creed.

Perhaps the most likely reason, though, is that because the Bible speaks of what Jesus has done for us in so many ways, the early church didn't want to limit it to just one. To restrict ourselves to one understanding, when Scripture does not, is scarcely to be holding the Bible in the highest regard.

Whatever the reason, the upshot is that to be a 'proper' Christian according to the foundational creedal confessions of the early church we are not required to believe and teach one particular way of understanding how, exactly, Jesus saved us.

The way that Christians have explained the atonement over the course of history has mostly been through 'picture language'— metaphors, models, or ways of picturing it or likening it— that 'made sense' to people at that particular time; ideas that they could relate to, in their context and cultural surroundings.[6]

Let's begin, then, by tracking the principal waypoints in that journey.

THE OLD, OLD STORY IN THE FIRST 1,000 YEARS

COVENANT IMAGERY

The word 'covenant' is found in the Bible over 300 times—the first time is in Genesis and the last time is in Revelation. Even when the word itself doesn't appear, it's always there as the backdrop, against which the story of the Bible is to be understood.

Our English word comes from a Latin word that means to 'come together,' to be 'brought together' and be 'made compatible.' Our verb 'to convene'—as in, 'arranging a convention' or 'a coming together'— is from the same root. The connection between covenant and atonement is therefore obvious.

Covenants were in use throughout the Ancient World for creating and defining social and political relationships. They had several standard features. As we quickly run through them, notice how well they describe and make sense of what God has done for us through Jesus in the 'new covenant.'

- A covenant created a relationship that didn't previously exist, usually between unequal partners.
- It was founded on, or in the light of, an historical event.

- It set out commitments—binding promises, made under oath—that each of the parties was making to the other, and the expectations and benefits that would flow from it.
- Finally, there was almost always some 'ritual act'—to 'seal' or 'ratify' the covenant—which was seen as essential to the fulfilment of those promises. Typically, that would be a sacrifice, with the sacrifice becoming the centerpiece of a covenant meal shared together.

Covenants typically involved a great and powerful king called the 'suzerain' graciously offering to enter a relationship with a weaker and lesser king called the 'vassal.' Covenants involved pledges and benefits, with adverse consequences for breaches. The vassal would pledge loyalty and obedience to the suzerain, while the suzerain would pledge to protect and care for the vassal. Under a covenant relationship, the enemies of the vassal would now be the enemies of the suzerain. An attack on the vassal would be an attack on the suzerain.

The nature of a covenant meant that the relationship had to be an exclusive one. The vassal king couldn't enter relationships with other surrounding kings without being guilty of infidelity and betrayal.

Covenant also had a 'kinship' dynamic to it. To enter into a covenant was to bring those who were previously or potentially enemies into the family circle. No wonder that throughout the Bible, and especially in the New Testament, we see relationship with God being described in sonship terms, in adoption terms, in joining the family terms, and in marriage terms. These are all picturing the radical change of status that comes with being included in a covenant relationship.

Covenant is the basis for God's relationship with his people throughout the biblical story. It would not therefore be in the least surprising for this to have been the way for Jewish Jesus-followers in the early church to have most easily understood Jesus' death on the cross—as a covenant-initiating sacrifice.[7] This is affirmed by Jesus choosing to die at Passover, rather than on the Day of Atonement. God's actions vis-à-vis Pharaoh were those of a suzerain in a covenant relationship acting on behalf of a vassal—rescuing them from their enemies, fulfilling his covenantal commitment in that extended family relationship. In Exodus 4.21, God says, 'Israel is my son—let my son go.'

In the Last Supper, Jesus was inviting his disciples into a covenant relationship, extending family status to them as his brothers (John 15.15). They were invited to share in a covenantal meal with him, breaking bread together, invoking the memory of that very first Passover where the lamb served as a covenant sacrifice; the daubed blood of the lamb marking out those who were under the protection of the divine covenant-maker.

In Luke 22.20, Jesus took the cup, saying, 'This cup is the new covenant in my blood, which is poured out for you.' We see also Paul's awareness of the centrality of covenant in framing what Jesus has done for us:

> For I received from the Lord what I also passed on to you: the Lord Jesus, on the night he was betrayed, took bread, and when he had given thanks, he broke it and said, 'This is my body, which is for you; do this in remembrance of me.' In the same way, after supper he took the cup, saying, 'This cup is the new covenant in my blood; do this, whenever you drink it, in remembrance of me.' For whenever you eat this bread and drink this cup, you proclaim the Lord's death until he comes. 1 Corinthians 11.23-26

Covenant, as the basis of God's relationship with his creation—even before the covenantal relationship with Israel—begins way back in early Genesis. The theme could hardly be more embedded in the biblical account. If we are looking for the earliest understanding of Jesus' mission and the function of the cross, in its most overarching sense, it would almost certainly be in and through covenant (certainly for the first Jewish believers). The new covenant in Christ 'mirrored' Israel's own covenantal history. It can clearly be seen as the final iteration in a series of covenants—like the passing of a covenantal baton in a relay—leading to the ultimate 'new' covenant heralded in Jeremiah 31.31, sealed with the ultimate covenant sacrifice.

Understanding the place of covenant in the Bible is foundational to understanding relationship with God and the nature and character of God. He is a covenant-making, covenant-keeping, and covenant-faithful God. He is not a covenant-cancelling, fault-finding and 'looking-for-technical-ways-to-get-out-of-it' God. His faithfulness to us and his promises to us are framed within the expectations of Ancient World covenants. As Psalm 110.4 says, 'The Lord has taken an oath and will not break his vow.'

The Gospel is presenting God's invitation into a covenant relationship. Jesus reaching out to the outsiders and the outcasts and the poor and the sick and 'life's failures' (in human terms) was radically covenant-extending. It was challenging the religious leaders' assumptions and definitions, of who was inside and who was outside the covenant boundaries.

Each of the many biblical models and metaphors picturing the atonement (including those we shall mention in a moment) is explaining one of the many benefits of being in the new covenant relationship through Jesus, signed and sealed by Jesus' covenantal sacrifice at the cross and remembered and reaffirmed when we participate in communion (the eucharist, or 'breaking bread'). God in Christ as the suzerain acts on our behalf as the vassal, to rescue us and deliver us from every enemy that threatens, harms, and enslaves us, his extended covenantal family. Our enemies become his enemies, including the enemies of sin, Satan, and ultimately, death itself.

But herein lies a dilemma … Identifying the earliest understanding, however powerful it may have been in biblical times, only gets us so far, when the notion of covenant is as good as lost to us in today's world. Even though it is perhaps the most biblical of all biblical ways of understanding the foundation of Christ's atoning work, we would need to work extremely hard to communicate it as the Gospel today.

Marriage used to be a good example (think of the solemn pledges the couple make to each other, and the wider familial coming together at the wedding breakfast) and it still offers echoes of that Ancient World notion, but its effectiveness is diminishing. Perhaps the best example nowadays, albeit one that is corporate rather than personal, is a treaty between nations that has the force of international law behind it. You may remember the furor in Parliament in the lead up to Brexit when it was suggested that the British Government was planning to break its treaty obligations. However, only the most optimistic evangelist is likely to think that presenting the Gospel in those terms will be persuasive![8]

All this is reminding us that simply being 'biblical' in how we tell the Old, Old Story is not enough on its own; being 'missional' as well requires that we pay equal attention to how our audience will be able to grasp that Old, Old Story. Thank God, therefore, that he has given us a rich palette of biblical colors from which to paint pictures of the atonement for people in today's world.

SACRIFICE IMAGERY

It might well be said that sacrifice offers the imagery that would have most easily framed Jesus' death for first-century Jewish believers, given its central place in Jewish worship within the covenant in Torah and the fact that sacrifices continued throughout the New Testament period (until the Temple's destruction by the Roman legions in 70 CE). However, a few brief observations on sacrifice may be helpful as background.

Firstly, in the New Testament period 'any religion without the practice of sacrifice would have been inconceivable.'[9] Christian appropriation of the imagery is not in itself remarkable; pagan sacrifice was widely practiced, too (often accompanied in Roman cities by idol worship and debauched behavior, widely condemned by the New Testament writers). Sacrifice was embedded in the culture and the psyche.

Secondly, Jewish sacrifices were of a wide variety of types and made for a wide variety of reasons, by no means just 'sacrifices for sin' (as many Christians assume). One crucial role was in covenant ratification (see 'Covenant Imagery'). Moreover, the priestly sacrificial procedures were complex, to say the least, with a range of Hebrew words for types of sacrifice and offerings.

Thirdly, surprising though it may seem, no-one really knows exactly how sacrifice was supposed to 'work' (the Ancient World rather took it for granted that it did); 'Far more can be said about what was done in sacrifice than about what the rituals meant to those who performed them'![10] It's interesting to reflect on Jesus as sacrifice in the light of the following:

> Sacrifice can initiate a state of affairs (e.g., priestly status, Leviticus 8-9), it can correct a state of affairs (e.g., sin, impurity), and it can maintain and strengthen a relationship (the peace offering). It can be argued that the central concern of the priestly writings is the creation, maintenance, and restoration of an ordered world. ... sacrifice has a crucial role in maintaining order and restoring the equilibrium when that order is disturbed. Both sin and impurity can be understood as generating disorder, a broad category which can apply to the personal and the impersonal, the unavoidable and the deliberate, the individual and the corporate. This is therefore one way to do justice to the range of faults for which sacrifices are prescribed. [11]

Finally, the sense in which we use the word 'sacrifice' today—as generous self-giving for the sake of others—is not inappropriate to use in relation to Jesus (he was certainly doing that), but we should remember that that is not its Ancient World meaning, which was 'a gift to God' (or gods, as the case may be). We will say more about sacrifice when we look at justice, crime, and punishment, and specifically, penal substitution.

SLAVE MARKET IMAGERY

As the early church grew and expanded into the gentile world, we see atonement being explained in other ways. One picture comes from the Slave Market, and another from the Battlefield.

In the Slave Market metaphor, Jesus paid a ransom price to set us free from being slaves to sin and death and Satan;[12] he 'purchased our freedom.' When we read in the New Testament about Jesus 'paying the price,' 'ransoming us,' or 'redeeming' us, that's what it's talking about. This is known as the Ransom Theory, and is biblically grounded in the following texts:

- The Son of Man came to give his life as a ransom for many— Matthew 20.28.
- Christ Jesus gave himself as a ransom for all people— 1 Timothy 2.5-6.
- Once you were slaves of sin, but now you are free from your slavery to sin, and you have become slaves of God instead— Romans 6 (various).

At least a third of the population in urban areas would have been slaves in the first-century Greco-Roman world. One of the main reasons people ended up in slavery in peace time was financial, because they couldn't pay their debts, so with nothing else left to sell they sold themselves (or in some cases, their children).

Colossians 2.14 says that Jesus 'cancelled the charge of our legal indebtedness, which stood against us and condemned us; he has taken it away, nailing it to the cross.' 1 Corinthians 7.23 says, 'You were bought for a price; do not become slaves of people.' In other words, don't sell yourself back into spiritual slavery.

We can only imagine how powerful ransom imagery would have been in that world, in picturing what Jesus had done to release us from slavery: paying the price, cancelling our debt, buying us back from the slave master, purchasing our freedom, and saving us from a life of enslavement.

BATTLEFIELD IMAGERY

The Battlefield way of explaining the atonement pictures Jesus winning a victory over the hostile cosmic powers that are the enemies of human life: sin and death, Satan, and the evil under which humanity is suffering. We call this theory *Christus Victor.*

Ephesians 4.8 says that when Jesus ascended on high, he led captivity itself captive. Hebrews 2.14 says that Jesus had to share in our humanity, so that by his death he might break the power of him who holds the power of death, that is, the Devil.

The cross is the pivotal moment when all of the damaging and destructive forces that had invaded this world go into reverse and begin their retreat. Just like when the snow begins to melt in Narnia and the power of the White Witch starts to fade.

Christus Victor would have made a great deal more sense prior to the Enlightenment because the pre-Modern world was very supernaturally aware. Essentially, everyone believed in God or the gods, and spirits and spiritual forces, and saw them as intrinsically involved in 'causing' everything that happened in the world. If you have no real scientific understanding of what makes things happen, why would you not? Since the Enlightenment, Modern people have given 'the supernatural' credit for almost nothing; pre-Modern people gave it credit for almost everything![13]

Both Slave Market imagery and Battlefield imagery can be seen in tandem in Colossians 2.13-15:

Ransom: He forgave us all our sins, having cancelled the charge of our legal indebtedness, which stood against us and condemned us; he has taken it away, nailing it to the cross.

Christus Victor: And having disarmed the powers and authorities, he made a public spectacle of them, triumphing over them by the cross.

'IN ADAM' AND 'IN CHRIST' IMAGERY

In the earliest drafts of the book, this section was not included! That's mainly because it's one of the hardest ways of explaining the atonement, because it begins with the idea of Adam and Jesus being 'representatives' of humanity as a whole (affecting us all for 'bad' in the first instance and for 'good' in the second); a way of thinking that's alien to our world. It eventually made the cut because (a) I increased the word count, (b) what it's saying about what Jesus did for us is actually rather important, and (c) with some thought and care given to reworking it in contemporary terms it can be very meaningful.

This way of picturing the atonement is properly known as 'recapitulation,' or 'interchange.' No doubt you can already see why it nearly didn't make it! Hardly catchy, are they? Let's get the technical stuff out of the way, and then I'll try to reshape it in language and pictures that will hopefully make more sense; material you might profitably be able to weave into a Gospel explanation.

'Recapitulation' means saying something again in a 'summing up' sense—like when we talk about 'recapping' a conversation. It also has a musical meaning—re-playing a section of a piece of music, typically as its pinnacle—and, a biological meaning, of an embryo going through the same development stages as its antecedents before it. This is the first aspect—technically known as 'Adam Christology'—in which Jesus reprises Adam.

'Interchange' does not so much mean an exchange as a merging, such as when two people meet up to share and meld ideas together. So rather than Jesus' work being a 'substitution,' as it's often referred to when we talk about atonement, interchange explains it in terms of a 'participation.' By entering our humanity as one of us and sharing in our human experience, Jesus transformed what it means to be human 'from within' for everyone who—in Paul's language—is 'in Christ,' rather than being only 'in Adam.' A scriptural basis for this is reflected in 'God made him who had no sin to be sin for us, so that in him we might become the righteousness of God.' 2 Corinthians 5.21.

This way of thinking about Jesus' atoning work emphasizes in the first instance the significance of the incarnation (God becoming man). That is not to diminish the cross; rather, it reminds us of the significance of the entirety of Jesus' mission and achievement, none of which should be left out or deemphasized—his incarnation, life, ministry, suffering, death, resurrection, and ascension.[14] The 'good news' of Jesus embraces and speaks to us through all of those aspects.[15] We can and should draw freely from every element in presenting the good news of Jesus today.

The atonement was first framed in this way by Irenaeus, in the second century. He saw Jesus as 'recapitulating' human life in himself, as the 'new Adam' or 'second Adam' that Paul speaks of in Romans 5.12-19 and 1 Corinthians 15.21-23; 45-49.[16] It's referenced in an old hymn written by John Henry (later, Cardinal) Newman, 'Praise to the Holiest in the Height':

O loving wisdom of our God!
When all was sin and shame,

a second Adam to the fight
and to the rescue came.

What humanity lost through Adam's disobedience was won back through Jesus' obedience, 'undoing' or 'reversing' what went wrong in human life. The divine plan to rescue humanity *from within humanity* was a 'recapitulation'—a repeating or replaying of the original creation, but with a different outcome.

In the fourth century, Athanasius put it like this: Jesus became as we are, so that we might become as he is. He pictured it as a restorative work on the damaged and tarnished *Imago Dei* (the Image of God in humanity), like an expert restorer repristinating a portrait on an oil painting, restoring it to its original condition.

Also in the fourth century, Gregory of Nazianzus said: 'What has not been assumed has not been healed; it is [only] what is united to his divinity that is saved.' In other words, Gregory was stressing the necessity, for our salvation, of Jesus the Son of God becoming fully human as we are, fully participating in our humanity (uniting divinity to humanity in himself). Hebrews 2 reflects this necessity: 'Since the children have flesh and blood, he too shared in their humanity so that by his death he might break the power of him who holds the power of death ... For this reason, he had to be made like them, fully human in every way, in order that ... he might make atonement for the sins of the people.'[17] (See verses 14-18)

How might we draw from this in ways that can make sense for an audience today?

Jesus became the first of a new kind of people of God, according to a new pattern, a new way of being human. The Apostle Paul pictures this by contrasting 'what Adam did,' with 'what Jesus did.' Romans 5 says that 'sin and death' came into the world through 'Adam'; when he exercised his freewill, he changed the course of human history. But the defeat of sin and death came into the world through Jesus when he exercised his freewill and changed the course of human history.

We should remember that 'Adam' is not just a reference to an individual man in the creation story (or Paul's writings), it's also (depending on the context) a generic reference to the human race.

When we read about 'Adam and Eve' we need to know that there's some wordplay going on here that would have been 'obvious' to the original audience, because the Hebrew word *'adam* is the word for 'mankind' or 'humanity.' So, the story is not just talking about one man and woman, it's talking about all of us. It's not just picturing what they were like and what they did and why—it's picturing what we're like and what we do and why. It's not just their story, it's our story too; a story that repeats itself again and again throughout human history. We can see ourselves in Adam and Eve, just as we can see ourselves in many of the other biblical characters, from Genesis onwards.[18]

In computer language, Jesus 're-booted' human life, pressing Control-Alt-Delete to restart it with a new version of the human operating system *in himself*, according to a new pattern of what it means to be human, with a new and different outcome for human life.

It's presenting 'A Tale of Two Stories.' The Gospel is God's invitation to change stories: to exchange the story written for our lives by the first Adam, for a story written by the second Adam. A new story that ends in life, instead of an old story that ends in death. By entering our human story—becoming like us, becoming one of us—Jesus transformed what it means to be human for all who are 'in him,' who choose to join him in his new version of the human story. He rewinds and then re-records the story, undoing 'what Adam did,' starting life afresh for all who are 'in Christ.'

Jesus' invitation is to join him in a new life born into the family of God. John 1.12 says, 'To all who received him . . . he gave power to become children of God.' Ephesians 1.5 says that 'God decided in advance to adopt us into his own family by bringing us to himself through Jesus.' To be 'born again' (in the classic phrase of John 3.16) is to start life again, in the image and likeness and outcome of Jesus in resurrection—instead of the image and likeness and outcome of 'Adam' in death.

These, then, were the principal ways of thinking about and explaining Jesus' work—what Jesus has done for us to bring about an atoned relationship between people and God—in the first 1,000 or so years of the Christian faith.

THE OLD, OLD STORY IN THE MEDIAEVAL & EARLY MODERN PERIOD

ANSELM'S SATISFACTION THEORY

Some may find it surprising, given how often we think of it in those terms today, that it's not until the eleventh century—1,000 years after Jesus—that we see the atonement being explained through legal imagery. In its first incarnation, it's a very particular form of legal imagery that is nigh on impossible for us to relate to today. It depends for its effectiveness almost entirely on the cultural context of mediaeval feudalism, rather than on the Bible—which makes it even more ironic that it should be the source for a theory of the atonement which became not only the one most favored by the Reformers (whose mantra was *sola scriptura*—'the Bible alone') but also the one most favored (if not also insisted upon) by their Reformed and Calvinist heirs to this day.

In mediaeval feudalism, all criminal acts were seen as an affront to the personal honor of the feudal Lord, because he was personally responsible for upholding law and order. Committing a crime, therefore, dishonored and shamed him personally, giving rise to a debt of offended honor that in mediaeval chivalry required 'satisfaction.' We see this pictured in costume dramas, when the stereotypical brave knight challenges the evil baron to a duel—throwing down the gauntlet, demanding satisfaction, to assuage the offended honor of a fair lady.

In the reign of William the Conqueror, the Archbishop of Canterbury was a man called Anselm. He borrowed this way of thinking to picture God as a cosmic version of the feudal lord. The theory ran that human sin had dishonored and shamed God, giving rise to a debt of offended divine honor that humanity was unable to satisfy. So it was, said Anselm, that Jesus satisfied that debt on our behalf with the infinite value of his life.

This may sound a bit weird to us, but then we don't live in the Middle Ages. Anselm appropriated this imagery, rooted in the mediaeval world, because it would communicate well within that culture. People would be able to say, 'I get that! That makes perfect sense.' Interestingly, though, there are no Bible verses we can offer to support it, because people didn't think like that in Bible times. It was a product of the way of thinking of mediaeval feudalism, that made sense to them, then.

Anselm is often said to be the first to explain the atonement in terms of what's called 'penal substitution' (of which more anon)—meaning that, at the cross, Jesus took our punishment for sin upon himself. But that's not actually what was happening here, because—in the feudal system—satisfaction was *the alternative* to punishment. Satisfaction *averted* punishment. There was only ever punishment if satisfaction was not achieved.

Anselm's thinking was certainly 'substitutionary'—namely, Jesus doing for us what we could not do for ourselves; acting for us, in our place—but it was not 'penal' substitutionary. All the best ways of picturing the atonement are substitutionary in that sense, but by no means does that make them *penal* as well. 'Substitutionary atonement' is *not* synonymous with 'penal substitutionary atonement'—Jesus being punished.

Similarly, if you hear the word 'satisfaction' being used in relation to penal substitution, as it sometimes is—for example, 'satisfying' God's wrath—please don't attribute that to Anselm. What he had in mind when he used the word was only that particular (if not also slightly peculiar) mediaeval feudal concept, of 'satisfaction of offended honor.'

ABELARD'S 'WONDROUS CROSS' THEORY

At around the same time as Anselm came Peter Abelard, the pre-eminent philosopher and theologian of the twelfth century, also famous as a poet and a musician.[19] Abelard argued that the problem with Anselm's thinking was the way that it pictures God—as aloof, demanding, easily offended and judgmental. He does not need to be 'bought off' (i.e., appeased) by some payment. Rather, said Abelard,

> The atonement was directed primarily at humanity, not God. There is nothing inherent in God that must be appeased before he is willing to forgive sinful humanity.
>
> Through the incarnation and death of Jesus Christ, the love of God shines like a beacon, beckoning humanity to come and fellowship.[20]

Abelard's way of picturing the atonement is known as Moral Influence; another phrase that's hardly catchy! It's perhaps best illustrated in the words of the old hymn, 'When I Survey the Wondrous Cross' (hence the reason I frame it that way). Rather than the cross effecting a change in God (enabling him to forgive), its power lies in effecting a change in us, as we stand in awe, wonder, and amazement that God himself would do such a thing for our sakes, revealing himself to us in that way. We are irresistibly drawn to him by this ultimate demonstration of 'love so amazing, so divine' that it 'demands my soul, my life, my all.'

This is a way of seeing the atonement—or perhaps more importantly, the nature and character of God that underlies the atonement—which is reflected in the Parable of the Prodigal Son, in Luke 15, where we see no legal imagery, no appeasement of anger (still less, no offended honor), and no punishment taking place in order for forgiveness and reconciliation to be made possible.

Simplified, the core difference between these two mediaeval ways of conceiving and explaining the atonement—Anselm and Abelard—is that Anselm's satisfaction theory sees the cross effecting a change in God toward humanity, whilst Abelard's moral influence theory sees the cross effecting a change in humanity toward God. The difference is often characterized as 'an objective' understanding versus 'a subjective' understanding. Many theologians would say—rightly in my view—that these should not be seen as being in opposition to each other; Jesus' work should be seen as both-and, not either-or.

THE REFORMERS' PENAL THEORY

Fast forward to the time of the Reformation, a few hundred years later. Martin Luther and John Calvin (who both trained as lawyers) were impressed by Anselm's starting point that divine justice 'had to' be satisfied. But the legal system in Europe had now changed. Feudal law had been replaced with a form of Roman law. So, the Reformers simply reworked the feudal model of Anselm's day to fit with the criminal justice system of their day, under which 'satisfaction'—to make punishment unnecessary—was no longer an option. According to the thinking of *that* legal system, for justice to be done, there now *had* to be punishment. And so was born the 'penal' understanding of the atonement.

Equally significantly, in those days the penalty—the legal sentence for crimes—was almost always physical violence, such as torture, bodily mutilation, hanging, burning alive and drowning. This was carried out in a public spectacle, to shame the criminal and frighten everyone else. The idea of the prison sentence as we know it today only came into being around two hundred years ago, following what we call penal reform.

Both civil crimes and religious crimes—like heresy—were treated the same way; there was no distinction.

For the Reformers, all these features of their culture's justice system shaped their conception of an equivalent divine justice system. As with Anselm, it helped people to be able to say, 'I get that! That makes perfect sense.' Just as Anselm saw Jesus fulfilling the requirements for justice to be done in his day—with God as the divine feudal Lord—so, too, the Reformers saw Jesus fulfilling the requirements for justice to be done in their day—with God as the divine courtroom Judge. While Anselm saw satisfaction as necessary, Calvin saw punishment as necessary. Both views were based on what 'justice being done' looked like in the world they lived in.

Today's Understandings of Justice, Crime & Punishment

Penal Substitution Today

If we were in the room together at this point, I would ask how you currently explain the Old, Old Story to people, or the version that you first heard. It's quite likely that it would have been based around penal substitution. Thanks to the very strong influence of Reformed theology in evangelicalism, many Christians have been told that there's 'only one way' to explain it, and that 'has to be' penal substitution, especially in a US context. And yet, from what we've already seen, patently it doesn't. Which is just as well, given that our understanding of what it looks like for 'justice to be done' today has changed again—just as it did in the transition from Anselm's era to the Reformers' era. Explaining what Jesus has done for us by framing it in a legal model of crime and punishment only 'works' if the legal model is one that society recognizes as fulfilling justice being done—one which instils, 'I get that! That makes perfect sense.'

In the Reformers' day, prison was where people were held before trial, or when they were waiting for punishment to be inflicted. It was only very rarely used as a sentence. Two hundred years ago, in England, over 200 offences were punishable by death. Nowadays, though, we have *no* offences punishable by death. Nor do we inflict sentences of physical violence on criminals. We no longer flog people or hang small boys for stealing a loaf of bread. We think the few countries that still do such things are barbaric, unenlightened, still living in the dark ages. We believe that punishment should be proportionate to the crime. Our contemporary values lead us also to believe in restorative justice and, wherever possible, the goal of rehabilitating offenders (as well as suffering the consequences of their wrongdoing by depriving them of their freedom for a period of time).

We still believe in justice and hence, we have no problem in principle with believing in a God of justice. One might even say that Postmoderns are especially concerned for justice. But what justice looks like to us is not the same as it looked to Anselm, Luther, or Calvin. What was 'obvious' in crime and punishment to them, and to the Ancient World that preceded them, is not what is 'obvious' in our world in crime and punishment today.

At the time of the Reformation, up to one-in-four of all convicted criminals was publicly executed, because in the worldview of the time this was 'obviously' right. There was no distinction between civil crimes and religious crimes. Calvin served as an expert witness helping to convict a heretic called Servetus. Calvin is famous for trying to get the sentence reduced to beheading with a sword or hanging, because that would be more humane than burning him at the stake ...

We can quite see how easy it would have been, two hundred plus years ago, to explain the Old, Old Story in terms of Jesus taking our punishment at the cross—the punishment that we deserve for breaking God's laws. But we can also see how hard it is to explain Jesus in those terms today, when our worldview of crime and punishment is very different.

Interestingly, it was religious groups—such as Quakers and evangelicals—that were at the forefront of achieving penal reform. This is more than ironic, when many evangelicals continue to explain the cross today in a way that entirely corresponds to the Ancient World thinking about crime and punishment that they helped to overturn.[21] In fairness, this usually comes about for two reasons. The first is because they quite rightly do not want to undermine God being a God of justice as well as a God of love (he most certainly is both). So far, so good. But then they make an unwarranted assumption that 'justice' must mean judicial punishment conceived in Ancient World terms. The second reason is not realizing that they are allowed to explain the cross in other ways instead (which is down to the strong influence of penal substitution within Reformed evangelicalism).

LAW COURT IMAGERY TODAY

Let's be clear: it's by no means inappropriate to continue to use a legal metaphor for explaining the Old, Old Story if we want to. And it's most certainly not inappropriate to say that each of us will be accountable to a God of justice for the way that we've lived. That is very much a given; it's an essential part of the story. But it *is* inappropriate to feel we must frame the story in terms of a legal system and approach to criminal sentencing that people no longer recognize. The same could be said, of course, for how people explain and present hell, which is heavily influenced by Dante's Inferno and mediaeval paintings.[22]

The reason all this matters for Christian mission is because if there are no wrongdoings (however great the crime) that deserve the death penalty in our legal system (still less, the brutal physical violence of the cross), then we have a bit of a problem explaining to people how every wrongdoing (however small the crime) deserves it in God's legal system ... before we then explain to them the 'good news'—that Jesus has taken that punishment for us, saving us from it. Good news that just happens to entirely depend for *being* good news on Ancient World thinking.

Some readers may be thinking at this point, 'But what about what the Bible says about penal substitution? Surely, if it's biblical, we're not at liberty to ignore it?' And that would be true. But firstly, we must remember that, as we have already seen, simply to be 'biblical' in how we tell the Old, Old Story is not enough on its own. Being 'missional' as well requires that we pay equal attention to our audience being able to grasp that Old, Old Story. To be 'evangelical' is to be properly conscious of both. God has given us a rich palette of biblical colors from which to paint pictures of the atonement for people so that we are not wedded to having to use one that does not communicate in a particular cultural setting—or communicate as well as it used to. Anselm's 'satisfaction' theory of offended divine honor, rooted in mediaeval feudalism—feudal lords, brave knights, dastardly evil barons, and fair maidens—is an obvious case in point.

For evangelicals, of course, what the Bible says is quite rightly crucial. And yet—to many evangelicals' surprise, when it's explained to them—there are relatively few verses presenting the Old, Old Story in those terms. Language of 'redeeming us,' 'ransoming us,' and 'paying the price' for us (to purchase our freedom from the slave master) all come from the Slave Market. They're not talking about penal substitution. The same is true when it comes to verses that speak of 'sacrifice.' Biblical sacrifices certainly included sacrifices for sin, but they were also made for a variety of other purposes, including sealing a covenant, thanksgiving, remembrance of God's great deeds of the past, communion with God, or simply a gift to God in response to God's goodness.[23] Sacrifice 'is a grander idea and does not in itself require a narrative of God's judicial wrath needing to be satisfied.'[24] Even in sacrifices for sin, the animal was not being punished. The point was never to make it suffer. Greater sin did not necessitate greater suffering being inflicted.

When we lay to one side all the verses about redeeming, ransoming, paying the price, and sacrifice, there's not a great deal left to support penal substitution. Yes, we can find it if we want to, but it's far from prominent and certainly not sufficient to require every other way of thinking about the atonement to either revolve around it or be subservient to it. As the theologian Steve Holmes concedes, writing as one who affirms penal substitution,

> Much of the language about the atonement in the New Testament could be understood in penal substitutionary terms if we had good reason to do so, but equally could be understood in other terms. When we read of Jesus 'redeeming' us, or 'paying the price' for our sin, if we already know from somewhere else that penal substitution is the right way to understand the atonement, then we can read these as different ways of describing penal substitution. When you look at writers arguing that penal substitution is the right way to understand the cross in the Bible, this seems to be what a lot of them do.[25]

As we noted earlier, it's very interesting that Jesus chose to die at Passover, which was focused on liberation, rather than the Day of Atonement, which was focused on sin.[26] Passover was celebrating the Exodus—the event that released Israel from captivity, oppression, and slavery to become the people of God. In Jesus' victorious life, death, resurrection and ascension, the enemies of human life and human well-being were defeated just as God had defeated Pharaoh. Framing the cross against a backdrop of Passover, as Scripture clearly does, speaks more of covenant imagery and *Christus Victor* imagery. The Passover sacrifice was not a sin offering. Quite aside from being pre-Sinai (before the giving of the Law that provided for sin offerings), there was no substitution going on. The function of the blood on the doorposts and the lintels was to mark out the people of God who were under his protection—quite literally, 'covered by' or 'under' the blood of the lamb. Paul in 1 Corinthians 5.7 speaks of Jesus in Passover lamb terms—'Christ, our Passover lamb, has been sacrificed.'

Even on the Day of Atonement, the scapegoat is not a substitute, it's not being punished, and it's *not even* being sacrificed. Leviticus 16 speaks of it as 'the goat that lives.'[27] John the Baptist speaks of Jesus in 'scapegoat' terms in John 1.29—'Look, the Lamb of God, who takes away the sin of the world!'

ATONEMENT IN THE BIBLE

Finally, we need to explain one more historical aspect. The New Testament Greek word for atonement is *hilasterion*, which has two distinct meanings.[28] One is to 'cleanse,' to 'take away,' or to 'cover' (sin). We call that 'expiation.' The Day of Atonement frames it in that way. The other is 'to appease the anger' (of a deity), making a payment to 'buy' their goodwill and to 'placate their wrath.' We call that 'propitiation.' Penal substitution frames it in that way.

Given these two options, the way that Bible translators choose to translate the word into English will depend on what they think is going on in the atonement—the nature of the human 'problem' that they think that the atonement was solving. Since it has those two, equally viable meanings, they're not simply translating 'word for word,' they're choosing their preferred interpretation as well (we must remember that translation is itself an act of interpretation).

For example, in rendering the word in 1 John 2.2, the NIV and the NRSV sit on the fence: 'He is the *atoning sacrifice* for our sins.' But the ESV insists: 'He is the *propitiation* for our sins.' While the RSV says no, 'He is the *expiation* for our sins.'

Other versions avoid being as specific as the ESV and the RSV, one way or the other (partly for very good reason—expiation and propitiation are hardly common words in everyday speech) but even then, they can't avoid their preferred interpretation showing through, often by adding to the text. For example: 'Jesus died in our place, to take away our sins' (ICB), 'He is God's way of dealing with our sins' (CEB), 'He gave his life to pay for our sins' (NIRV), and he's 'the means by which our sins are forgiven' (GNT). Finally, the Living Bible paraphrase doesn't hold back on what it thinks: 'He is the one who took God's wrath against our sins upon himself.' The Living Bible is even more ideologically driven when it encounters the same word in Romans 3.25. The NIV and the NRSV again go with 'a sacrifice of atonement,' but the Living Bible goes the whole hog: 'God sent Christ Jesus to take the punishment for our sins and to end all God's anger against us ... the means of saving us from his wrath.' If you hadn't encountered the Reformed doctrine of penal substitution before, you have now—and all generated from one Greek word plus a bit of ideology thrown in!

So, *what was* going on at the cross? Was it *expiation*—cleansing, taking away, and covering? Or was it *propitiation*—appeasing God's anger, placating his wrath, and buying his goodwill? Feel free to choose, since there is no clear, single right answer generated by the word itself (you can even explain it as both if you wish). That said, it will be obvious which of the two will be more likely to enable people today to say, 'I get that! That makes perfect sense!' Our choice, ultimately, will need to be decided on theological grounds; what we believe most makes sense in the light of the nature and character of the God we know, revealed uniquely to us in Jesus. Tempering our decision also on missional grounds—what is and isn't going to make sense to our unchurched audience.

Perhaps we should give a last word to the place in Scripture where we first come across the Hebrew equivalent of the word, which is *kapporet*, in Exodus 25, where it's referring to the pure gold cover on the ark of the covenant. Martin Luther translated it as the *gnadenstuhl* ('seat of grace'), which is traditionally rendered 'mercy seat' in English Bibles (see Hebrews 9.5).

2

THE OLD, OLD STORY IN
A POSTMODERN WORLD

TODAY'S CULTURAL CONTEXT OF
POSTMODERNITY

M ANY CHRISTIANS HAVE BEEN told that Postmodernity is 'the enemy,'
and it's not difficult to see why some feel that. They're worried
about worldly thinking infiltrating the church, declining standards in
personal morality, creeping 'liberal' values in which 'anything goes,'
and aggressive challenges to what they see as 'biblical truth.' We don't
have space here to examine all of this in detail, so a few observations
will have to suffice.[29]

How people in a particular place and time, in a particular era and
socio-cultural setting, see what's 'obvious' to them about life is called
a 'worldview'—society's commonly-held view of how their world is.
These are not opinions as such, they are shared 'obviouses' that are
taken to be *so obvious* that no-one questions them; no-one thinks about

them; no-one needs to articulate them, and still less, for the most part, to debate them. They're just 'the way things are.' The shared features of a worldview are so taken for granted that they're almost invisible to us, like the air we breathe, or the water we swim in. As they say, 'A fish does not know what water is, because nothing else has ever occurred to it.' Worldviews are extremely hard to 'step out of,' to see the world from an entirely detached perspective; nigh on impossible, in fact.

Essentially, from a Western world perspective (and at risk of slight oversimplification) there have been three worldview eras: the Ancient World, from when time began until sometime from the 1500s onward; the Modern world (that we call 'Modernity') from then until around the 1950s onward; and the Postmodern world, from then to now. Currently in the West, Modernity and Postmodernity are overlapping, with the former retreating and the latter ever-increasing (especially amongst those born from the 1980s onwards).

Sometimes Christians will talk about a 'biblical worldview' (envisaging something to be pursued, or at least admired). On one level this is commendable—we 'know what they mean'—but on another level, it will mean endorsing if not copying some rather problematic features of the Ancient World worldview. Since God chose to give the Bible to us through human writers who were immersed in that particular worldview context—in turn, writing to people who fully shared that worldview—the Bible is by no means immune from us needing to pick out some 'cultural bones' from the divinely inspired text for today. That does not make it flawed; rather, it was an essential feature if it was to make sense to its original audience.

There are two key points about worldviews for our purposes here. The first is that no worldview is intrinsically 'Christian' (any more than any period of history is or was). They all have their good and bad features. Christians have been concerned about 'the spirit of the age,' declining moral values, and creeping liberalism, in eras well before anyone had ever heard of Postmodernity (even the New Testament writers were concerned). Defining something called a 'Christian worldview' will be elusive, given the very nature of worldviews. It will at a minimum require us to be able to critique our own worldview, including our own assumptions as to what's 'obvious' (and, at times, what's 'obviously right' and 'obviously wrong'). This is especially the case for anyone who has grown up within Modernity. A particular danger is that it's all too easy to unwittingly anoint the Modern worldview as if it is the biblical gold standard against which Postmodern thinking and values should be judged (clearly, it's not—Modernity's ways of thinking have no direct line of continuity with Jesus and the early church). To see the weaknesses in our own worldview is extremely difficult, though, because it seems so 'obviously' right to us.

The second key point is that far from being simply an enemy to be fought and resisted, Postmodernity offers lots of opportunities from a missional perspective compared with the Modernity that preceded it. Today's lack of familiarity with Christianity as an institutional religion means we have more of a blank canvas to work with, and correspondingly less embedded religious baggage ('churchianity') to clear away. There is little, if any, of the animosity toward church and religion that was an obstacle for mission in the West (certainly in Britain) during much of the twentieth century. Postmoderns are very interested in spirituality and very happy to talk about it. A disdain for consumerism and the excesses of capitalism, a concern for fairness and justice in the world, and the importance of people's personal stories and experiences are all features that are intrinsically friendly toward the Gospel (provided, of course, that we resonate enough with those things ourselves to embrace them). Postmoderns certainly understand relational breakdown and the need for reconciliation—which is at the heart of atonement—because they see and experience it so persistently in their families and friends.

However, the relatively recent but significant and fast-paced shift from the 'obviouses' of Modernity to the 'obviouses' of Postmodernity means that as evangelicals who tend to be more mindful of unchanging truth than changing culture, we will need to work far harder. The ideas, concepts, and language that we've relied on to frame the Gospel in Modernity will not work so well in Postmodernity. Apologetics—meaning, how we 'sell' people the truth about God—will need a rethink. Reasoned, rational arguments based on proof and evidence are the mindset of Modernity flowing from the Enlightenment—the Age of Reason, the Age of Science, and the Age of the Machine (in which we've become accustomed to thinking scientifically and mechanistically about all manner of subjects). These features of Modernity's worldview became the tints in the lenses through which Modern people perceive the world, Christian faith, and the Bible.

The claims that we make for the authority of the Bible and for Christianity as a metanarrative (namely, a single, overarching, controlling story that is and must be true for everyone, everywhere, in the exact same way) will not be effective if framed in those terms.[30] But why lead with concepts that are hardest for your audience to relate to? Postmoderns are understandably skeptical toward claims to intrinsic authority (especially, moral authority) by institutions and their leaders, both religious and secular. They are unlikely to think that just quoting a Bible verse as 'the Bible says' settles anything, so we shouldn't expect it to. This skepticism is not just toward religious claims, but equally to those of institutions, big business and government (not least because they perceive longstanding historic patterns of cover-ups, hypocrisy, vested self-interest, and prioritizing profits over people).

Postmodernity is well-known for denying there is such a thing as 'absolute truth'—in other words, 'your truth isn't necessarily my truth'—which at first glance appears to be deeply problematic for a Christian faith that rests on the unique and universal truth of Jesus. But

I think we can all agree that whilst there must surely be such a thing as absolute truth—certainly from God's perspective—none of us right now has an absolute grasp of that absolute truth. We don't comprehend it absolutely. We have diverse personal experiences of it (illustrated, if not also validated, by the presence in Scripture of four separate eyewitness accounts of Jesus' life). In that sense, while all genuine encounters with Jesus will be harmonious, reflecting different aspects of one whole, the 'truths' they reflect will not always be identical. We see in the Gospels that Jesus would speak different elements of truth to different people; his message was not always framed the exact same way. His central message of the Kingdom of God had many elements, inviting (and challenging) people in different ways; it still has, and it still does. Ask a roomful of people for their testimonies of how they first became a Christian and that diversity will be evident. It seems that the God who is himself, unquestionably, absolute truth is also the God who says 'I will be who I will be' to each of us individually, as he chooses.[31] The wind of the Spirit—the one who guides us into the truth—blows wherever he wishes (John 3.8; 16.13).

Might it simply be the case that Postmoderns find Modern Christian truth claims lacking sufficient humility?

How do we avoid the great fear—of *changing* the Story? It starts with being aware of the extent to which the way we have been telling the Story might itself have become wrapped in the ways of thinking to which we have become accustomed since the Enlightenment. It means being sufficiently theologically aware that we can revisit the language and concepts and metaphors that we use to convey the Gospel while remaining faithful to the heart of Scripture. Simply quoting verses from the NLT instead of the KJV will not cut it—we're talking about far more than that. It means being generous toward how Postmodern people think and feel, and what's important to them, and why. This enables us to focus on the positive aspects—the values that we can affirm in Postmodernity—rather than just what we find problematic. It is well past time to lay to rest the perception of Christians being far better known for what they are against than what they are for.

For people in our congregations who grew up in Modernity, the language and concepts and metaphors that we use to convey the Old, Old Story in Postmodernity may not sound like the Old, Old Story they're used to. They may find it disquieting not to be hearing certain words and phrases, or certain Bible verses quoted, that they've grown accustomed to expecting in a 'proper' Gospel talk. But this must happen, since to continue to tell the Old, Old Story in a distinctly Modern way will not be persuasive for a Postmodern audience. And in any event, we shouldn't be aiming to please those who know Jesus already—we're aiming to reach those who don't. We should not be surprised at having to re-think how we tell the Old, Old Story in a Postmodern world any more than the first Jewish disciples had to figure out how to tell it in a gentile world. Or Anselm, in a mediaeval world. Or Luther and Calvin, in an Early Modern world. And so on. Overseas missionaries have long since understood the need to speak the cultural language of the people amongst whom they are working, just as much as they need to communicate in their spoken and written language. This realization has been far less apparent in home mission.

In a Postmodern world, we also need to allow space for questions, mysteries, and even some 'I don't know,' without feeling that to admit to that will fatally undermine the Christian message. In Modernity, any uncertainty was seen as a weakness, and hence, it had to be either denied or resolved by presenting persuasive logical arguments and factual proofs; in Postmodernity, it is simply recognizing something that to most people nowadays is stark-staring obvious. Given God's limitlessness versus our human finitude, surely it could not be otherwise. An element of mystery, puzzle, and paradox is not in itself a flaw; indeed, it may be more intrinsic (and even, more attractive) to Christian faith than we realize.[32]

THE GOSPEL IN POSTMODERNITY

JESUS-CENTRIC GOOD NEWS

Just to be clear, what we are seeking to do is to convey the good news of Jesus in ways that are *both* authentic to the biblical account *and* responsive to Postmodern ways of thinking. The goal is for our audience to be able to say, 'I get that! That makes perfect sense.' This requires, as with any journey, that we 'start where people are at.' One helpful approach is to adopt a story-focused approach, centered in Jesus.[33]

It's interesting—and for Modern evangelicals, somewhat disconcerting—that in none of the four Gospels do we find a single, overarching definition of *the* Gospel in one place. As a result, evangelicals have ended up producing their own summary versions, selecting bits and pieces from different verses and passages, and stringing them together to say, 'This is the Gospel.' (Google 'What is the Gospel?' and you'll see what I mean.)

The danger in such an exercise is that the results can appear to be 'filling in what Jesus chose to leave out'—especially when the Apostle Paul is used to do that. If I may be crude for one moment, to assemble a Gospel using selected biblical proof-texts picked from here and there runs the risk of creating the equivalent of Frankenstein's monster sourced from a mortuary's spare body parts. Selecting bits and pieces from different verses and passages is perfectly OK in one sense; provided, of course, that we're starting with the right bits and pieces, and the best bits and pieces. But the outcome may be reducing the Gospel down to something that fails to do justice to all the ways in which Jesus is good news—reducing it to only certain ways in which Jesus is good news. Or, ending up with something that might be accurate to a statement of faith but makes no sense at all to our unchurched friends.

In the Gospels themselves, Jesus seemed to explain the good news in different ways to different people at different times; at a minimum, he appeared to focus on different elements with different people. But what we can say is that *he never once* explained it as the classic twentieth-century evangelical 'Four Spiritual Laws'—a very selective and very 'Modern' framing of the Gospel drawn from a few choice proof-texts.[34] Despite its popularity in the evangelical world, only in John's Gospel—and even then, only in one conversation—do we see Jesus speaking about the need for someone to be 'born again.' Not that this is untrue, or that we can't use it, but we should perhaps not over-work it.

In the very first verse of the first chapter, Mark begins his Gospel with: 'This is the beginning of the good news about Jesus.' However, he doesn't then start defining what the good news is (still less, borrowing from things Paul wrote), because *the whole of his Gospel* was the good news about Jesus. As it was also for Matthew, Luke, and John. For them, the good news of the Gospel was everything that Jesus said, everything that Jesus did, and everything that Jesus was and is—then, and now. The Gospel is all of the ways in which Jesus was good news to the people who experienced him. The ways in which we see Jesus welcoming someone, receiving someone, being kind to someone, loving someone, forgiving someone, and explaining what God is like to someone—all of that is the good news.

Even where we see Jesus challenging people—and especially when he challenged the religious leaders, and the people in power—that is part of the good news as well. Because 'good news people' don't turn a blind eye and stay silent when 'bad news' is hurting people and harming people. It's why we can't ignore social justice and issues like poverty, racism, inequality, injustice, and suffering (not least, if we want Postmoderns to take us seriously).

James, the brother of Jesus—who you'd think would know Jesus pretty well, and who would know what the Gospel is as well as anyone—said this:

> Suppose a brother or a sister is without clothes and daily food. If one of you says to them, 'Go in peace; keep warm and well fed,' but does nothing about their physical needs, what good is it? In the same way, faith by itself, if it's not accompanied by action, is dead. James 2.14-17

We are called to 'be' good news, to 'embody' good news, and to 'do' good news, not just to preach good news. Our calling is 'both/ and' not 'either/or.' It is not being a 'wooly liberal' to see the 'good news' through the lens of Jesus' mission statement in his first recorded sermon, in Luke 4.18-19, in which he echoes Isaiah 61:

> 'The Spirit of the Lord is on me,
>   because he has anointed me
>   to proclaim good news to the poor.
> He has sent me to proclaim freedom for the prisoners
>   and recovery of sight for the blind,
>   to set the oppressed free,
>   to proclaim the year of the Lord's favor.'

The reason it's so important for us to read the Gospels, and to know the stories in the Gospels, is because the ways in which Jesus was good news to people when they encountered him then are the same ways that he wants to be good news to people when they encounter him now. Jesus is the same yesterday, today and forever (Hebrews 13.8):

- Jesus will welcome us now, the way he welcomed them then.
- Jesus will receive us, the way he received them.
- Jesus will say to us the kind of things he said to them.
- Jesus will love us, understand us, offer forgiveness to us, and have a heart of compassion toward us, in the same ways that he loved, understood, forgave, and had a heart of compassion toward them.
- The ways that Jesus explained what God is like are the ways he wants us to understand what God is like.

In other words, Jesus will be good news in our lives in the same ways that he was good news in their lives. He will also challenge us the way he challenged them. But once we've experienced being welcomed by Jesus, and loved and understood and forgiven by Jesus, then we will surely welcome being challenged by Jesus as well, because we will know that it's for our best;[35] to help us become all that he wants us to be.

As we're reading through the Gospels, we should be noticing all of the good news in the stories, such as:

- The way that Jesus was good news for the woman caught in adultery (John 8).
- The way that Jesus was good news for the Samaritan woman at the well (John 4).
- The way that Jesus was good news for the criminal crucified alongside him (Luke 23).
- The way that the Father was good news in the Parable of the Prodigal Son (Luke 15).
- The way that the Shepherd was good news in the Parable of the Lost Sheep (Matthew 18).

- The ways that Jesus was good news for the oppressed, and the victims.
- And the ways that Jesus was *bad news* for the oppressors, in stories like the Rich Man and Lazarus (Luke 16)—that's good news, too!

So, let's get reading. Let's look out for all of the ways in which Jesus was good news, personally model those ways, and pass them on. Let's ask the Holy Spirit to show us the equivalent people and people groups in society today—those whom Jesus would be reaching out to in similarly radical ways now—the people who would be featuring in today's 'Jesus stories,' if he were here with us bodily.

One of the really interesting things in the Gospels is how rarely Jesus' good news seems to have come with any strings attached. For some reason, he doesn't seem to have been particularly bothered about proving his doctrinal orthodoxy by caveating everything all the time—which of course was one of the things that upset the religious people, and still does. You may say: 'But what about the woman caught in adultery? Didn't Jesus say to her, 'Go and sin no more'?' That's true, he did. But only after she'd experienced his love, understanding, kindness, and compassion; only after he'd said, 'I don't condemn you,' and stopped other people condemning her as well (it's easy to miss how radical, how generous, and how welcoming Jesus was being). It's a perfect example of what Paul says in Romans 2.4: it's the kindness of God that leads to repentance; not repentance that leads to the kindness of God.

Another thing we see is *how unexpectedly* Jesus was good news to people. The ways that he welcomed people, received people, spent time with people, was kind to people, loved people, forgave people, was genuinely interested in people (as people, not projects) and explained what God was like to people were all 'breaking the rules.' Or perhaps I should say, 'rewriting' the rules. Not because God had changed, but because people's understandings and expectations of what God was like needed to change—Jesus embodied 'the gold standard' and remains the gold standard.

What God is like—and the things that are most important to him—are at the heart of Jesus' arguments with the Pharisees. The Pharisees certainly believed in a loving God, but it was always conditional: 'You need to be doing the right things so that you can be loved and accepted and forgiven by God.' But Jesus was saying, 'You've got it the wrong way round. Once you understand how much you're already loved and accepted and forgiven by God then you'll want to be doing the right things.' The Pharisees tended to see 'loving God' as fulfilled through loving the law of God, about which they were passionate; Jesus said, no, first and foremost, loving God is fulfilled through loving the people of God, for whom he was passionate.

We need to be careful not to be making the same mistake that they did: starting our Gospel—our 'good news'—with sin rather than grace. Adding on conditions and caveats to what Jesus said. Explicit or implicit 'ifs' and 'buts' and 'provided this' and 'provided that.' The Parable of the Prodigal Son is a classic example. If that is an authentic picture of how God the Father loves, welcomes, and forgives us as prodigals, then we've no business adding back in supposedly vital theological information—still less, additional requirements—that Jesus chose to leave out. Despite the *sola gratia* ('by grace alone') of the Protestant Reformation,[36] too rarely in practice are we as gracious as God is—generously dispensing unmerited favor to people who don't deserve it—in which the key phrase is, *who don't deserve it.*

Yes, of course, Jesus was concerned about people living right and doing what's right, and yes, of course, sin and righteousness are things he took seriously. And so, too, should we. But grace—lots and lots of it—comes first. It's funny how the more religious a person is, the more of a problem they seem to have with that; the more they seem to want to start with sin. If that upsets you, think about it. Then go out and prove me wrong!

SHARING THE GOOD NEWS

OK—read this next paragraph extremely carefully. Maybe more than once:

If all of the ways in which Jesus is good news in the Gospels is *the* Gospel ... If all of the ways that we see Jesus welcoming someone, receiving someone, being kind to someone, loving someone, forgiving someone, and explaining what God is like to someone are 'the good news' ... then anything that reduces that down, anything that stops short of it, or understates it, or limits it, or undermines it, is something less than the whole Gospel.

So, we don't want to be doing that. But there's a practical problem: the four Gospels are some 82,000 words, which is about twenty sermons, or four books like this one. So, when we want to explain the 'good news' to people, we can't just say 'read the Gospels.' We need to summarize it in some way. But if we're going to explain how Jesus is good news in just a few sentences, or in just a few ways, we shall have to be extremely careful which aspects we choose—which aspects we're going to start with and start from.

Fortunately, the Gospels themselves offer us a veritable smörgåsbord, an All You Can Eat Buffet (depending which metaphor you prefer), of different 'good news' to choose from. And of course, it's not just the Gospels. We've got the whole of the rest of the Bible as well, although we shall need to make sure that we're always reading it through our 'Jesus lenses.'

How, then, might we go about that?

One option is to try to do it the 'theological' way—aiming to make sure we're including all the right phrases, all the right verses, and all the right words, so that it's technically accurate and leaves nothing out.

And that's fine. But dare I say, it's unlikely to be the most effective way for the people we're wanting to reach. We're not trying to pass a theology exam here. The more theological that most of us try to be, the more religious sounding we usually end up.

A better option is to start with what Jesus means for us, in our own lives; how we've personally experienced Jesus as 'good news.' And so long as that's a good reflection of the Jesus we see in the Gospels, then it's a really good approach. It may be what Paul had in mind when he talked about 'my Gospel' in Romans and 2 Timothy. Postmodern people love real-life stories. They love seeing what someone's 'truth' looks like when it's lived out in a person's life. 'Maybe what you've found to be true for you can be true for me, as well' is a Postmodern-friendly approach that does not undermine truth as absolute (it's what we used to call 'my testimony').

And a third option is to start with whatever aspects of the 'good news' of Jesus are going to work best for the person we're speaking to. We ask the Holy Spirit to show us what 'bad news' looks like for them, so that we can explain how Jesus is good news in their bad news—as he surely wants to be. This is not at all the same as saying that we 'make up' Gospels to order, to suit people. We don't need to—the good news of Jesus is 'wide and long and high and deep' enough already, because the love of God is (Ephesians 3.18). It's simply starting where people are at, which seems to be what Jesus himself did. What any good communicator would do, in fact. We are the ones who need to make sure we're not limiting its width and length and height and depth in how we explain it.

The problem with the 'theological' approach on its own is that we're in danger of offering Jesus as the answer to questions people aren't asking. There's no point saying Jesus is the answer to questions people used to have—or even, ones that they ought to have. There's no point saying Jesus is the solution to problems they don't recognize.

If we're going to explain the Gospel to people, we must do so using words, concepts, and starting points that they can grasp—that 'make sense' to them in their own life experience. The 'technical stuff' can come later.

When I ask people from an unchurched background about their stories of how they first became Christians, it's astonishing how rarely good, sound theological explanations (centered in 'what happened at the cross') seem to have featured at the outset. I would suggest to you that this is not because their first encounters with Jesus were invalid, or the person who led them into that relationship did a terrible job, but because that is the reality for so many people: the Holy Spirit does what he does in leading them into truth that makes sense to *them*. Yes, the Spirit guides into *all* truth (John 16.13), but he's happy to start with *their* truth. God is allowed to do that if he wishes; so, let him. As I say, the 'technical stuff' can come later.

SIN, GUILT, AND SHAME

Years ago, a very common way of presenting the Gospel was to make people feel guilty about what sinners they were. It was successful in a world in which people learned Christianity at school, quite likely went to church when they were younger, and grew up knowing deep down that there was a God—even though they knew they weren't following him as they ought to be. Western society was a guilt-based culture, in which the consequences of wrongdoing were punishment, and the primary need was forgiveness. The goal for evangelists was therefore to get people to see that they were guilty sinners who needed to repent, enabling forgiveness to be received, and thus the punishment that people implicitly knew they deserved averted. This is where the idea of 'revival' came from—the Holy Spirit 'bringing back to life' (stirring up) a knowledge of God and a sense of guilt, and fear of punishment, that was latent inside people. And in years gone by, that worked a treat. The success of Billy Graham in his heyday is a classic illustration.

But the problem is that in the Postmodern world these features are no longer present as they used to be. There's nothing there, latent inside people, to revive, so our definition of 'revival'—what we expect revival to look like, and what will bring it about—needs to change too. As Alan Mann rightly says, 'Individuals no longer live with a sense of sin and guilt in the way that evangelists would wish them to in order to successfully communicate the atoning work of Christ.'[37] Our revival model needs to change.

Postmodernity is now a shame-based culture. If that statement doesn't immediately make sense to you, it's worthy of some further research.[38] Shame in Postmodernity bears a relationship to the cultural world of the Bible and also to traditional Asian honor-shame cultures, but it's not quite the same. A New York Times article by David Brooks, 'The Shame Culture,' explains some of its features in a simple way:

> In a guilt culture you know you are good or bad by what your conscience feels. In a shame culture you know you are good or bad by what your community says about you, by whether it honors or excludes you. In a guilt culture people sometimes feel they do bad things; in a shame culture social exclusion makes people feel they *are* bad.
>
> ... the omnipresence of social media has created a new sort of shame culture. The world of Facebook, Instagram and the rest is a world of constant display and observation. The desire to be embraced and praised by the community is intense. People dread being exiled and condemned. Moral life is not built on the continuum of right and wrong; it's built on the continuum of inclusion and exclusion.

This creates a set of common behavior patterns. First, members of a group lavish one another with praise so that they themselves might be accepted and praised in turn.

Second, there are nonetheless enforcers within the group who build their personal power and reputation by policing the group and condemning those who break the group code. Social media can be vicious to those who don't fit in. Twitter can erupt in instant ridicule for anyone who stumbles.[39]

The lesson here is that when evangelists rely solely on a Modern guilt-based Gospel—when they start from sin, as individuals having 'done bad things,' and what sinners they are because of those bad things, and how deserving of God's wrath that makes them—before then playing the trump card, 'But don't worry, because Jesus is the solution to that problem,' many in their audience are simply not going to 'get it' in the way that they used to years ago. *Whether* we're sinners, and guilty before God, is not the point. Of course we are, and of course the Gospel is God's remedy for that guilt. But once again, this is about *where we start from*. It's about winning people. It's about how the Gospel relates to problems they currently feel, like shame, not to ones they don't feel.

In case this sounds like being 'soft on sin,' it's not. It's actually taking sin more seriously, because sin affects human beings in so many ways. We live in a world that's been broken and damaged by sin. Sometimes we experience it as perpetrators—we 'do' sin—and sometimes we experience it as victims—we 'suffer' sin, through what sin and sinful people do to us. Some people experience sin in one capacity more than the other. Sin is more than my own personal list of sinful acts— it's also the impact and consequences to myself and others of living in a sin-infected world. Our Gospel must be big enough—and sensitive enough—to allow for sin in all its effects on human life. Jesus died for sin, and to save us from sin, and to win the victory over sin, in all the ways that it affects us. Jesus may just as well have been speaking about sin personified as a robber when he said in John 10.10, 'The thief comes only to steal and kill and destroy; I have come that they may have life and have it to the full.' Sin is an enemy that robs people of life in all its fullness.

Evangelicalism tends to want to simplify everything possible, which can be both good and bad. Simplification is commendable when it helps people to grasp something, but not if it involves reducing something down to a point where it fails to adequately reflect the whole truth. When 'the problem' of sin is reduced down to a list of personal acts that I have committed and 'the solution' is presented simply as getting personal forgiveness to avert punishment, then way too much is being left out. Reductionism has distorted both problem and solution to a point where it can easily become a caricature: 'If you would like to be forgiven and go to heaven when you die, just say 'amen,' after I pray this prayer ...' What's more, it's a particularly Modern reductionism. Yes of course the cross brings forgiveness, but it also:

- Brings healing and cleansing.
- Restores right relationship with God, with others, and with myself.
- Changes us from enemies of God to friends of God.
- Brings us peace; restoring *shalom* and wholeness.[40]
- Invites us into his family—the people of God.
- Deals with our shame and exclusion.
- Reverses the damage done by sin in all its facets.
- Brings hope and purpose.
- Leads to eternal life.

Interestingly, when the Apostle Paul talks about sin, it's mostly in the singular—sin, rather than 'sins'—sin as a hostile power. Paul speaks of it in terms of a personified enemy that wants to rule and reign in our world—to deceive us, control us, and enslave us—reminiscent of way back in Genesis 4.7, where God says to Cain: 'Sin is crouching at your door; its desire is to have you …'

Sin is a difficult word nowadays; there's no question that we need new language for it. If we are to use the word at all (and especially so when speaking to unchurched people) we absolutely must define it for them and define it well, in terms they can personally related to.

One way to explain it in non-religious words is in terms of selfishness. Sin is embedded in society because selfishness is embedded in society. It's our typical, default reaction, especially when we're threatened or under pressure. The very worst kinds of sin can be characterized as hyper-selfishness—selfishness that's 'out of control'—that doesn't care whether it hurts people, or how much they get hurt, in us pursuing things that we want. Sin is an enemy agent that infiltrates our values, our behaviors, our relationships, and our ways of thinking. It embeds itself in our institutions, our politics, and our social structures. It seeks to infiltrate our justice systems and create injustice systems. It wants to make us guilty, and it wants to shame us. The thief that Jesus spoke of in John 10.10 wants to steal and kill and destroy body, soul and spirit— physically and psychologically—to shame and to exclude, as well as to tempt and make guilty.

Seamlessly switching metaphors, sin is like a virus, one that's highly infectious. None of us is asymptomatic; we're all infected, and we all infect others. Sin is the first—and most troubling—global pandemic, not least because it continues to evolve into ever-new variants, impervious to society's best secular vaccines.

On the cross, Jesus took the sin of the world upon himself. He defeated the power of sin. He bore the consequences of sin. He paid the price for sin. The cross is the 'good news' solution to the problem of sin in all of its features and all of the ways it affects us and our world—

our institutions, our economic systems, our culture, our values, our ambitions, and our relationships—not just our individual, personal guilt. On the cross, Jesus bore our shame and our exclusion—the cross was a shaming event.[41]

'Just-as-if-I'd-never-sinned,' once I've 'prayed the prayer,' is crass reductionism. It's not a biblical definition of justification, it's a caricature of justification. That is not the Gospel, it's a Pythonesque parody of the Gospel. When Zacchaeus encountered Jesus in Luke 19, he didn't say 'Now that I've said sorry it's all forgiven and forgotten. It's just as if I'd never sinned. Heaven here we come.' No, he said, 'Here and now I'm giving half my possessions to the poor, and if I've cheated anybody out of anything, I will pay back four times the amount.' To which Jesus responded, 'Today salvation has come to this house.' That is not a 'cheap gospel,' it's a very expensive gospel—experienced by someone who truly 'gets it.' I don't recall seeing that in the Four Spiritual Laws, any more than I remember the Rich Young Ruler featuring—that young man to whom Jesus, when asked 'What must I do to get eternal life?' famously replied, 'Go, sell everything you have and give to the poor, and you will have treasure in heaven. Then come, follow me.' (Mark 10.17-23; cf. Matthew 19.16-22) Time for a Fifth Spiritual Law, perhaps ...?

'Repent' and 'repentance' are words that have also suffered from chronic reductionism. They're often deployed today simply to mean 'saying sorry' for your past sins, to enable them to be forgiven, when the underlying meaning is deeper and broader. It means 'changing your mind,' 'changing your way of thinking,' and 'turning around'— you were going one way in life, now choose to turn around and go in the opposite direction. Change the things you love, the things you're devoted to (aka, 'what you worship'), and the things you're doing, insofar as they're incompatible with being a child of God. Repentance is not just a one-time event to close the deal on our personal salvation, it's a present-tense continuous practice as we seek for our lives to become increasingly aligned with Jesus and his Kingdom. And once more, it's relationally focused rather than transactionally focused.

Finally, in our passion to share the grace of God with perpetrators, we must not be insensitive to the suffering of those they've harmed, for whom it will not instantly be 'just as if they'd never sinned.' The crude expectation we sometimes hear that a victim of adultery, or marital violence, or systematic abuse, has to 'forgive and forget' because the perpetrator has 'said sorry' (to them and to Jesus) needs to be radically re-thought, both pastorally and theologically; starting with grace and sensitivity to the parties harmed, rather than with dogma, ideology, and forgiveness proof-texts. The way we explain the Gospel must be good news to the victims *at least as much* as to the perpetrators. Preserving a marriage must never be at the cost of perpetuating abuse. Marital abuse is covenantal unfaithfulness every bit as much as sexual adultery.

THE GOSPEL AND RELATIONSHIP

There are so many ways that we can explain what Jesus has done; so many ways we can shape the story for our audience. The Bible is a treasure chest of images and ideas. As we've seen, that's because there are so many ways it pictures 'the human problem' to which Jesus is the solution. But perhaps the aspect that people are most likely to recognize and identify with in today's world is broken relationship.

Everyone knows that there's a loneliness and an emptiness that comes from the absence of relationship. We were made to be social people, involved in each other's lives. As God said way back in Genesis 2.18, it's not good for people to be alone.

Not only is there a chronic emptiness in our lives if we are cut off from human relationships—as the Covid lockdowns have exemplified—so too there's an emptiness if we don't have a relationship with God. It's like there's a God-shaped space inside every person, a spiritual vacuum that only God himself can fill.

Mending a broken relationship is called reconciliation. In Colossians 1, Paul explains what Jesus has done for us as a reconciliation; something we could not achieve for ourselves:

> ... through him, God reconciled everything to himself. He made peace with everything in heaven and on earth by means of Christ's blood on the cross. This includes you who were once far away from God. You were his enemies, separated from him by your evil thoughts and actions. Yet now he has reconciled you to himself through the death of Christ in his physical body ... Colossians 1.20-22

Not only has Jesus done this for us, but he has also given us 'the ministry of reconciliation'—he has committed to us 'the message of reconciliation.' (2 Corinthians 5.17-19) Notice in the passage that this reconciliation extends beyond reconciling 'you to himself' into 'everything in heaven and on earth.' Righteousness is not something ethereal, it's something concrete. God's righteousness reigns 'when everything in life is right'— and, it's relationally centered: right with God, right with people, right with ourselves, and right with creation. It starts with receiving 'the free gift of righteousness' through Jesus (Romans 5.17) through his 'abundance of grace,' and it continues with us aligning our lives with living in the fullness of that righteousness in all of its facets (Romans 6.18-19).

I would highly recommend that relationship and relational restoration features prominently in our explanations of the Gospel in today's world. Pretty much everyone, in every family, has experienced relationships breaking down—people who once were close no longer talking to each other. People for whom things have come between them, often not knowing how to go about repairing the damage, and whether it even can be repaired.

At the same time, let's not allow our presentation of the good news ever to be monochrome; there is no need to overly rely on just one aspect or image. For example, let's weave together relational restoration with 'changing life stories' imagery, or adoption imagery, or family imagery (though keep in mind that not everyone's experiences of 'father' and 'family' will have been positive ones). And let's never forget the Postmodern significance of 'shame' and 'exclusion' for our Gospel message. Healing the emotional and psychological damage caused by sin that causes someone not to be 'right with themselves' is part of Jesus' atoning work.

THE MEANING OF 'SALVATION'

It used to be commonplace for street-corner preachers to target passers-by with the question, 'Are you saved, brother?' But what does 'salvation' and being 'saved' mean, exactly? Those being so accosted may well ask, especially today. Such language is likely to sound very old-fashioned and religious. But clearly, what it's pointing to is important. The very word 'Jesus' means 'God is salvation.'

Already we've seen that both the human 'problem' and the divine 'solution' in Christ is multi-faceted—it means far, far more than a reductionist offer of 'going to heaven when you die' (or put more crudely, having a 'Get Out of Hell Free' card in our back pocket ready for when our time comes). Yes, it includes that, but it's more than that. The heart of eternal life is relational, and it begins in the present. As Jesus said, 'This is eternal life: that they know you, the only true God, and Jesus Christ, whom you have sent.' Eternal life is about a *quality* of life in relationship with God through Jesus—a foretaste of the life of the age to come in the present, beginning now. It's not just speaking of a *quantity* of life that starts upon physical death.

This fuller, deeper, and richer meaning is confirmed when we know a little more about the New Testament Greek words, that come from the *sōtēria* word group (*sōzō* is the verb).[42] They're used well over 150 times. The range of meaning embraces being 'kept from harm,' 'rescued' (from danger or death), 'healed,' 'liberated,'[43] and 'made whole.' In the Old Testament, the central Hebrew idea is 'freedom from what restricts and binds'; the other principal meanings are bringing 'peace' or 'wholeness,' and 'covenant deliverance.'[44]

Jesus' healings were not 'to prove he was God,' nor even just acts of compassion (though they were that too, of course). They also served to bring those who were excluded back into the community (e.g., in the healing of lepers). The healings in Jesus' ministry were foreshadowing the full and complete healing of all of God's creation in the age to come. Salvation is a comprehensive idea that embraces all of life and all of creation being 'right'—everything as it should be. By no means is salvation referring simply, in a negative sense, to what we're saved from.

At the same time, our own experience of the Christian life will tell us that not all of these biblical features of 'salvation' and 'being saved'—not all of 'the promises' in Scripture—will be experienced now in their full measure. This is not at all due to people's 'lack of faith,' as a quick read of Hebrews 11.35-39 will make abundantly clear. Nor was it in Paul's failure to receive healing (2 Corinthians 12.8)— surely a 'man of faith' if ever there was one.

There is a clear tension in biblical promises between 'the now' and the 'not yet.' As Christians, we need to keep the two in balance—the blessings of salvation already, in this present age, *versus* the blessings of salvation that will only be fully realized in the age to come. Biblical promises do span both, but overstating ('over-promising,' or 'over-selling') how much is available to us now causes great harm, especially when 'faith' is invoked as the means to receive it, in so-called 'name it and claim it' teaching.[45] The best biblical ways to think of the present benefits are as either a 'deposit' (with the full consideration to follow), or 'first fruits' (which are the same as the full harvest in quality but not yet in quantity).

WHAT WE'RE SAVED FOR

The Gospel is God's invitation through Jesus to join him in his work, for the *Missio Dei* (the mission of God) to impact the world. It's not simply about getting individuals saved—getting 'butts into Heaven,' as someone once put it (slightly crudely, but nonetheless memorably). The Gospel is also his invitation for us to be his transforming agents within society, something that many Postmoderns are passionate about. We're not saved *by* good works, but we are saved *for* good works, as the Bible makes abundantly clear (e.g., Ephesians 2.10).[46]

Modernity was individualistic to the point of selfishness. Modernity's way of conceiving the Gospel was individualized to the point of selfishness. We must not unwittingly make the same mistake, which we easily could, since Postmodernity has the same potential. The Gospel is always personal, but it should never be individualistic or individualized. It may start with me, but it should never stop with me.

Personal transformation through the Gospel is a launch pad for joining in the entire mission of God, modelled on the life and teaching of Jesus.

Unlike in Modernity, Postmoderns may struggle to see their own personal sinfulness as the core 'human problem,' if it's first presented to them in those terms. But they do see that there *is* a human problem, and that it's wide-ranging in its effects. The Gospel of Jesus as the solution is also wide-ranging; we must not artificially limit it.

We should not underestimate the power of attraction of a Gospel message to join Jesus in his mission now, as well as to join him in heaven later. His invitation to the disciples to 'Come, follow me' did not mean simply enjoying Jesus' company and learning more and more about him (though that is not to be denied or demeaned). It was also joining him in 'doing the works of him who sent me' (John 9.4) and 'doing what he sees the Father doing' (John 5.19). Serving a God of justice means being people of justice. Loving God means loving everything and everyone God loves. And righteousness includes being right with God's creation—this planet, our world—where our calling is to be stewards and curators, not rapists and pillagers.

Naturally, our calling is majorly focused on introducing people into relationship with Jesus—'making disciples,' as Jesus put it in his final words in Matthew's Gospel, in Matthew 28 (as distinct from 'making believers,' one might add)—but it's also aligning ourselves with the broader terms in which Jesus characterized his mission at the start of Luke's Gospel, in Luke 4.18-19. Interestingly, those two passages 'bookend' his mission (first sermon, and parting words). Our anointing with the Spirit (v.18) is for the same purposes as Jesus' anointing: being good news to the poor, bringing freedom to prisoners, sight to the blind, setting the oppressed free, and proclaiming 'the year of the Lord's favor.'

Evangelicalism has been wary of diluting its perceived priority—of preaching a 'spiritual' Gospel—by a so-called 'social' Gospel. But in Jesus' mind, the two seemed inseparable. Indeed, he had very strong words for those who 'spiritualized-away' things that mattered to him (consider Matthew 7.21-23 in the light of Matthew 25.31-45). What looks to have happened is that some parts of evangelicalism have unwittingly bought into the Enlightenment worldview that the Church's role is simply to superintend personal religion—as a private, inward matter for individuals—and stay out of the affairs of wider society in the public space. This has then conspired with evangelicalism's traditional fear of unwittingly lapsing into 'works righteousness'—confusing being saved *for* good works with being saved *by* good works.

The way that we live and love and serve God and one another as a community of Christians should be modelling 'Kingdom' to the world—what life together looks like under the rule and reign of God. We should be a 'society within society' (yet never detached or aloof from society), in which the presence of the Spirit of God makes a visible and tangible difference. The early Church Father, Tertullian, visualized pagan Romans looking at the church and saying, 'See how they love one another!' in dramatic contrast to the society around. Our light shining as individual Christians is one thing ('this little light of mine, I'm gonna let it shine'), but the light of a 'city set on a hill' (all our lights together) is something else entirely.[47]

If the expression of the Body of Christ that we are extending Postmodern people an invitation to join (a local church) is actively committed to Jesus' mission to transform lives and transform society through loving and serving its local community, they will see an added purpose to their faith. The church should model both social action and promoting justice and fairness in society—not for 'political' reasons, but for 'spiritual' reasons, rooted in the biblical story.

A Gospel invitation that seems to be mostly about me and what I get out of it, especially when it's centered in what happens when I die (scarcely at all to do with making a difference to the world I live in right now) will increasingly be seen as unattractive. In 'loving God' and 'loving neighbour'—Jesus' (single) Great Commandment— love must be a 'doing' word, not just an inwards feelings word. Postmoderns want to help change the world, so let's give them something to devote their time and passions to, beyond (just) saving souls.

Reading this section, you may be thinking, 'I'm not sure what some of this has got to do with the Gospel.' But what if it has everything to do with the Gospel? Unchurched Postmoderns might not have amassed much Bible knowledge, but I think they readily resonate with what Jesus said should characterize his authentic followers: 'By their fruit you will recognize them.' Matthew 7; Luke 6; John 15.

CLOSING THOUGHTS

The Bible offers us a rich palette of colors with which to paint pictures of how Jesus saves us, drawn from his incarnation, life, teaching, death, and resurrection—what that salvation looks like, and its significance and impact for our world. The biblical story offers a smörgåsbord—an All You Can Eat Buffet of good news to choose from. We may start wherever we like, whatever will be most effective in enabling those who do not know Jesus to say, 'I get that! That makes perfect sense.'

The way of thinking that we've become used to in the last few hundred years of Modernity says that there must be one core, foundational truth on any subject (hence the belief that one version of the Gospel—usually, penal substitution—must be 'the one').[48] But in Postmodernity the 'structure' of truth no longer needs to be pictured that way. The image of a building's foundation can be interchangeable (replaced, even) with the image of a spider's web, whose multiple anchor points all contribute to the structure's strength and stability. Both building and web are equally valid structures, they're just different structures.

The multiple ways in which Jesus' saving work can be understood and personally experienced is one easy way for evangelicals to reflect Postmodern ways of thinking, with a firm biblical basis—one that offers a bigger Gospel, with many more access points for people to 'get it.' Not only does our biblical mandate grant us that license, but our missional mandate requires that we take it up.

Will we, over time, want all new followers of Jesus to understand all of the ways in which he saves us—all of the pictures and aspects of atonement? Yes, of course. Need we insist on a particular one as their initial access point to grasping hold of that salvation? No, of course not. Think of it like a large building, with many sides and many different entrances. People can initially access that building through whichever is easiest and closest to them. Over time, they will, of course, want to become familiar with all sides and all entrances (though they can still be allowed to retain a favorite). Alternatively, think of it as a gemstone, where the more facets there are, the more light comes through, and the more valuable it is.

By all means invite people into a relationship with Jesus through a penal substitutionary doorway for the Gospel if you wish. But let's just be sure that we're inviting them through the entrance that is easiest and closest to them, rather than the one that we personally prefer.

C S Lewis was, of course, completely right when he said that 'A man can accept what Christ has done without knowing how it works,' and 'The thing itself is infinitely more important than any explanation that theologians have produced.'[49] Jesus is to be known and experienced, not merely theologized about! And yet, the fact that we don't need to explain everything doesn't mean we don't need to explain anything. There is an 'Old, Old Story' of salvation through Jesus that needs telling.

The challenge is to be sharing the good news of that 'Old, Old Story' in new, new ways that will *both* make sense to people *and* remain faithful to the biblical account centered in Jesus in which that good news is found. This will mean much more than just copying Anselm's way, the Reformers' way, or even, Billy Graham's way. To be authentic to our mission—to one day hear the words, 'Well done, good and faithful servant'—requires that we rise to meet that challenge. How privileged we are to be the current custodians of that 'Old, Old Story,' called to articulate it afresh for today's world.

ENDNOTES

1 'I Love to Tell the Story,' published in 1869, is one of two hymns deriving from the poem, 'The Old, Old Story,' written by Katherine Hankey, an English Anglican missionary and nurse who was a member of the evangelical Clapham Sect. Its refrain was added (and the hymn set to music) by William G Fischer. The lyrics may be found at: https://evang.hymnal.net/en/hymn/evang/1064#1 (accessed 26 May, 2021). The second hymn was, 'Tell Me the Old, Old Story.'

2 https://news.gallup.com/opinion/polling-matters/324410/religious-group-voting-2020-election.aspx (accessed 23 March, 2022).

3 Bebbington is a leading historian of evangelicalism and culture, particularly in relation to Great Britain. He speaks of these four features as 'a quadrilateral of priorities that is the basis of Evangelicalism.' David W. Bebbington, *Evangelicalism in Modern Britain: a history from the 1730s to the 1980s* (London: Routledge, 1999), 2-3. It is probably the wide diversity of the many streams within Evangelicalism that leads to his quadrilateral being so often cited as defining its irreducible common features. On evangelicalism generally, and especially from a US standpoint, see also the work of American historians Mark Noll and George Marsden.

4 Bebbington, *Evangelicalism in Modern Britain*, 275.

5 J N D Kelly, *Early Christian Doctrines* (Peabody: Prince Press, 2003 edition), 163.

6 This was also the case for Israel's relationship with God pre-Christ, though that is beyond the scope of this book.

7 For more on Ancient World covenants as the foundational framework for understanding Jesus' mission, and his sacrificial death as covenant-initiating, see Stephen Burnhope, *Atonement and the New Perspective* (Eugene: Pickwick, 2017). A covenant was always 'sealed' or ratified through a sacrifice, which then became the centrepiece for a familial meal shared by the covenant parties (cf. John 6.54; 56).

8   International treaties were the basis for military intervention on behalf of Kuwait when Saddam Hussein invaded in 1990 (though one cannot but observe the significance to the West of Kuwait's oil production as well).

9   See 'Sacrifice and Sacrificial Offerings,' in *The Anchor Yale Bible Dictionary*, vol. 5 (New Haven: Yale University Press, 2008), 886.

10 Martin J Selman, 'Sacrifice in the Ancient Near East,' in Roger T Beckwith and Martin J Selman (eds.), *Sacrifice in the Bible* (Carlisle: Paternoster, 1995), 89.

11 Philip P Jenson, 'The Levitical Sacrificial System,' in Beckwith and Selman (eds.), *Sacrifice in the Bible*, 32.

12 The word 'Satan' comes from the Hebrew, while 'the Devil' comes from the Greek.

13 It is interesting that in Postmodernity an interest in the supernatural (and 'spirituality') has returned—a welcome reaction to disillusionment with coldly rational, mechanistic, scientific, secular Modernity.

14 A further element intrinsic to Jesus' achievement is his obedience, which rarely gets a mention in popular discussion of the Gospel and atonement. See e.g., Romans 5.19; Philippians 2.8-10; Matthew 26.39; 42.

15 It's easy to unwittingly overemphasize 'the cross' to the exclusion or diminution of the other aspects of Jesus' work (an obvious example of which is that without the resurrection, the cross is simply noble martyrdom). When Paul speaks of 'the cross,' I think he is often using it as shorthand (technically, as a synecdoche—a figure of speech in which a part of something is used as a reference to a greater whole—such as 'Whitehall,' for the British Government, or 'Washington,' for the US Federal Government). This would correspond to how Paul sometimes appears to use 'circumcision'—for example, in speaking of the 'party of the circumcision' in Galatians 2.12. Torah was obviously about far more than circumcision (it included *inter alia* food laws, Sabbath, temple worship and festivals), but circumcision was its central and most dramatic covenantal symbol—as indeed, in its own context, is the cross.

The cross is the pinnacle of Jesus' mission, the ultimate demonstration of God's love, in the ultimate covenant sacrifice. But let us not detach it and isolate it; the cross only fully makes sense when it's properly contextualized.

16 On 'interchange in Christ,' 'participation in Christ,' and 'Adam Christology,' see Morna D Hooker, *From Adam to Christ: Essays on Paul* (Eugene: Wipf & Stock, 2008).

17 On the necessity of Jesus being fully human as well as fully divine, see Stephen Burnhope, *How to Read the Bible Well: What It Is, What It Isn't, and How to Love It (Again)* (Eugene: Cascade, 2021), chapter 9, Was Jesus Superman?

18 Burnhope, *How to Read the Bible Well*, 46.

19 'Peter Abelard,' in Stanford Encyclopaedia of Philosophy, https://plato. stanford.edu/entries/abelard/ (accessed 27 May, 2021).

20 Paul R Eddy and James K Beilby, 'The Atonement: An Introduction,' in Beilby and Eddy (eds.), *The Nature of the Atonement: Four Views*, (Downers Grove: IVP Academic, 2006), 19.

21 Note, too, that this also corresponds to how the nature and duration of hell is often conceived (as eternal divine punishment).

22 For more on the traditional picturing of hell, see Burnhope, *How to Read the Bible Well*, 141-67.

23 Colin E Gunton, *The Actuality of Atonement* (Edinburgh: T&T Clark, 1988), 120.

24 Stephen Motyer, 'The Atonement in Hebrews,' in Derek Tidball, David Hilborn and Justin Thacker (eds.), *The Atonement Debate: Papers from the London Symposium on the Theology of Atonement* (Grand Rapids: Zondervan, 2008), 137.

25 Stephen R Holmes, *The Wondrous Cross: Atonement and Penal Substitution in the Bible and History* (Milton Keynes: Paternoster, 2007), 43.

26 The Day of Atonement (also known as 'The Day') was the annual festival on which the sanctuary was cleansed of impurities and the Israelites' sins

were figuratively 'sent away' (removed to the wilderness, 'outside the camp') through being laid upon the scapegoat. See 'Day of Atonement,' in *Anchor Yale Bible Dictionary*, vol. 2, 72-76.

27 Leviticus 16.20-22. What's happening in the scapegoat ritual is reminiscent of Psalm 103.12: 'As far as the east is from the west, so far has he removed our transgressions from us.'

28 The Hebrew is *kapporet*, referring to the place of atonement.

29 For more on worldviews and Postmodernity, see Burnhope, *How to Read the Bible Well*, 81-108.

30 Whether Christianity *is* a metanarrative that is true for all is not the point. In *The Postmodern Condition*, Jean-Francois Lyotard famously defined Postmodernity as 'incredulity toward metanarratives.' Wisdom therefore says, 'start somewhere else' than arguing this point.

31 Exodus 3.14, where the Hebrew can be rendered either 'I am who I am' or 'I will be who (or, what) I will be.'

32 Obvious examples include 'When I am weak, then I am strong' (2 Corinthians 12.10) and 'The greatest among you shall be your servant.' (Matthew 23.11).

33 Rather than a more proposition-centered approach, which is often drawn more from Paul's letters.

34 See https://campusministry.org/docs/tools/FourSpiritualLaws.pdf (accessed 18 March, 2022).

35 It is notable (if not also sobering) that Jesus' rebukes were almost invariably directed toward the religious, and especially religious leaders. A study of the Gospels looking out for the instances is illuminating.

36 The 'five Solas' are *sola scriptura* (Scripture alone), *solus Christus* (Christ alone), *sola fide* (faith alone), *sola gratia* (grace alone), and *soli Deo gloria* (glory to God alone).

37 *Atonement for a 'Sinless' Society: Engaging with an Emerging Culture* (Bletchley: Paternoster, 2005), 4. Republished by Wipf & Stock in a second edition (Eugene: Cascade, 2015). Mann's deployment of 'sinless' is not intending

to refer to a society *without* sin, but rather one that *does not see itself in terms of the category* of sin.

38 Mann's *Atonement for a 'Sinless' Society* is one place to start, but quite 'theological' (it was his Masters' dissertation). A short New York Times article by David Brooks, 'The Shame Culture,' offers a helpful overview, available at https://www.nytimes.com/2016/03/15/opinion/the-shame-culture.html. This in turn draws from a longer article by Andy Crouch, 'The Return of Shame,' originally written for *Christianity Today*, available at http://andy-crouch.com/articles/the_return_of_shame (both accessed 29 March, 2022).

39 Brooks, 'The Shame Culture.'

40 The Hebrew word *shalom* is inadequately translated as 'peace.' It speaks holistically of wholeness and completeness, of everything in life being right—when the world is all as it should be. It's the goal for new creation pictured in Revelation 21.

41 Hebrews 12.2.

42 'Soteriology' is the word for our theology of salvation.

43 'Salvation,' in *The Anchor Yale Bible Dictionary*, vol. 5, 910.

44 Carl W Wilson, 'Salvation, Save, Saviour,' in Everett F Harrison, Geoffrey W Bromiley and Carl F Henry (eds.), *Wycliffe Dictionary of Theology* (Peabody: Hendrickson Publishers, 2000 edition), 469.

45 For an excellent small booklet on the heresy that is 'word-faith' prosperity gospel teaching, see Pentecostal theologian Gordon D Fee, *The Disease of the Health & Wealth Gospels* (Vancouver: Regent College Publishing, 2006).

46 'For we are his workmanship, created in Christ Jesus for good works, which God prepared beforehand, that we should walk in them.' (cf. James 2.14-26).

47 'You are the light of the world. A city that is set on a hill cannot be hidden.' Matthew 5.14.

48 The technical term for which is 'foundationalist epistemology.'

49 C S Lewis, *Mere Christianity* (London: HarperCollins, 2002 edition), 54-55.

Lightning Source UK Ltd.
Milton Keynes UK
UKHW011536280822
407897UK00002B/562

9 781399 921329